Dreaming of Elsewhere

Dreaming of Elsewhere

Observations on Home

ESI EDUGYAN

XCLC
CANADIAN LITERATURE CENTRE
CENTRE DE LITTÉRATURE CANADIENNE

 THE UNIVERSITY OF ALBERTA PRESS

Published by

The University of Alberta Press
Ring House 2
Edmonton, Alberta, Canada T6G 2E1
www.uap.ualberta.ca

and

Canadian Literature Centre /
Centre de littérature canadienne
3–5 Humanities Centre
University of Alberta
Edmonton, Alberta, Canada T6G 2E5
www. www.arts.ualberta.ca/clc

LIBRARY AND ARCHIVES CANADA
CATALOGUING IN PUBLICATION

Edugyan, Esi, author
        Dreaming of elsewhere : observations on
home / Esi Edugyan.

(Henry Kreisel memorial lecture series)
Issued in print and electronic formats.
ISBN 978-0-88864-821-1 (pbk.).—
ISBN 978-0-88864-838-9 (pdf).—
ISBN 978-0-88864-836-5 (epub).—
ISBN 978-0-88864-837-2 (kindle)

        1. Edugyan, Esi—Travel. 2. Home—
Psychological aspects. I. Canadian Literature
Centre, issuing body II. Title. III. Series:
Henry Kreisel lecture series

PS8559.D795Z465 2014   C813'.6
C2013-908395-2
C2013-908396-0

First edition, first printing, 2014.
Printed and bound in Canada by Houghton
Boston Printers, Saskatoon, Saskatchewan.
Copyediting by Peter Midgley.

The University of Alberta Press is committed to
protecting our natural environment. As part of
our efforts, this book is printed on Enviro Paper: it
contains 100% post-consumer recycled fibres and
is acid- and chlorine-free.

The Canadian Literature Centre acknowledges
the support of the Alberta Foundation for the
Arts for the Henry Kreisel Lecture delivered by
Esi Edugyan in April 2013 at the University of
Alberta.

The University of Alberta Press gratefully
acknowledges the support received for its
publishing program from The Canada Council
for the Arts. The University of Alberta Press also
gratefully acknowledges the financial support
of the Government of Canada through the
Canada Book Fund (CBF) and the Government
of Alberta through the Alberta Multimedia
Development Fund (AMDF) for its publishing
activities.

Canada   Canada Council   Conseil des Arts
for the Arts   du Canada

Albertan
Government

*Photographs on pages 2–3, 12–13, and 26–27
by Esi Edugyan.*

For Kofi and Abena
and as ever, for Steven.

FOREWORD

The Henry Kreisel Lecture Series is the flagship event of the Canadian Literature Centre. The series originated in 2007 shortly after the creation of the CLC, which was made possible thanks to a leadership contribution from Edmonton's respected biblio-phile and patron of the arts, Dr. Eric Schloss. Every year since the inaugural lecture, the return of spring is ushered in with a widely-attended public address given by one of the country's most respected, talented, and internationally acclaimed authors. The Henry Kreisel Lecture is an event where the mission of the CLC is represented eloquently as it unites readers, writers, students, professors, and people from all spheres within the various cultural communities of Edmonton in their shared passion for a culture that is never more alive than when it is experienced as such: immediate, vibrant, diverse, and bristling with vital questions.

The CLC is extremely proud to welcome Esi Edugyan's elegant, heartfelt, and insightful lecture as part of this prestigious series that has, throughout the years, become a distinctive home to original pieces by Canada's top writers. Edugyan's erudite obser-vations on the fate of "home" in a post-colonial world is preceded by Lawrence Hill's reflection on the contemporary autodafé and the persistence of censorship; Annabel Lyon's musings on the challenges of representing women in antique times; Eden Robinson's insights on community and inspiration; Dany Laferrière's thoughts on exile in the francophone world; Wayne Johnston's text on the pitfalls of history; and Joseph Boyden's considerations on place, citizenry, exclusion, and social oppression. Together these lectures offer a portrait of the diversity and vitality of Canadian culture in the early twenty-first century. They illuminate how the work of the author, perhaps today more than ever, is a public endeavour that plays an active role in the evolution of society. The authors in the

Henry Kreisel Lecture Series speak to all of us. Some are explicitly attached to the Canadian landscape and experience, others find their inspiration elsewhere. But they all share a concern about what it means to live in a world where borders have become increasingly mobile and intangible. The book you hold in your hands is the latest addition to this exceptional collection of cutting-edge literary thought in Canada.

The Henry Kreisel Lecture Series was founded to honour the memory of a foremost Canadian intellectual. Author, University Professor and Officer of the Order of Canada, Henry Kreisel was born in Vienna into a Jewish family in 1922. He left his homeland for England in 1938 and was interned in Canada for eighteen months during the Second World War. After studying at the University of Toronto, he began teaching in 1947 at the University of Alberta, and served as chair of English from 1961 until 1970. He served as Vice-President (Academic) from 1970 to 1975, and was named University Professor in 1975, the highest academic award bestowed on faculty members by the University of Alberta. Professor Kreisel was an inspiring and beloved teacher who taught generations of students to love literature and was one of the first people to incorporate the immigrant experience to modern Canadian literature. He died in Edmonton in 1991. His works include two novels, *The Rich Man* (1948) and *The Betrayal* (1964), and a collection of short stories, *The Almost Meeting* (1981). His internment diary, alongside critical essays on his writing, appears in *Another Country: Writings by and about Henry Kreisel* (1985).

The generosity of Professor Kreisel's teaching at the University of Alberta and his influence on modern Canadian literature inspires the CLC in its public outreach, research pursuits, and continued commitment to the ever-growing richness of Canadian literatures. The Centre embraces Henry Kreisel's no less than revolutionary focus on the knowledge of one's own literature. The

CLC advocates for understanding the complicated and difficult world that informs Canadian writing, a world that can be simultaneously bettered and transformed by such works.

DANIEL LAFOREST
Director, Canadian Literature Centre
Edmonton, February 2014

LIMINAIRE

Les conférences Kreisel constituent l'événement le plus en
vue du Centre de littérature canadienne. La première d'entre
elles a eu lieu en 2007, dans la foulée de la création du CLC
l'année précédente grâce au don directeur du bibliophile illustre
edmontonien, le docteur Eric Schloss. Chaque année depuis, le
retour du printemps est devenu synonyme de ces conférences
très populaires offertes par certains des plus illustres et talentueux
auteurs au pays. L'événement incarne au mieux la mission du CLC
puisque s'y réunissent lecteurs, écrivains, étudiants, professeurs, et
membres des diverses communautés de Edmonton autour d'une
passion partagée pour une culture vivante, mouvante, et traversée
par des questionnements cruciaux.

Le CLC est fier d'accueillir cette année Esi Edugyan avec un
texte élégant, subtil et chargé d'émotions qui vient enrichir la série
des conférences Kreisel déjà forte de textes originaux offerts par
les meilleurs auteurs canadiens. L'approche érudite du sentiment
d'appartenance à l'époque postcoloniale adoptée par Edugyan
s'ajoute ainsi aux réflexions de Lawrence Hill sur les autodafé
contemporains et la persistance de la censure, aux considérations
de Annabel Lyon sur la représentation de la féminité antique, aux
intuitions de Eden Robinson sur la communauté et l'inspiration,
aux pensées de Dany Laferrière sur l'exil dans la francophonie, au
texte de Wayne Johnston sur les périls de la fiction historique, et
aux propositions de Joseph Boyden quant au lieu, à l'identité, et à
l'exclusion sociale. Ces conférences offrent ensemble une image
éloquente de l'ouverture et de la vitalité de la culture du Canada
au XXIe siècle. Elles montrent en quoi le travail de l'écrivain
joue un rôle vital dans l'évolution de la société. Les auteurs des
conférences Kreisel s'adressent à chacun d'entre nous. Certains
s'attachent explicitement à l'expérience et à la réalité canadiennes;

d'autres trouvent leur inspiration ailleurs. Mais chacun partage
un intérêt vif pour ce que peut signifier vivre dans un monde aux
frontières de plus en plus mobiles et poreuses. Le présent livre est
le plus récent de cette collection qui s'impose désormais comme
un espace privilégié de la pensée canadienne contemporaine.

Les conférences Kreisel se consacrent annuellement à
perpétuer la mémoire du Professeur Henri Kreisel. Auteur,
professeur universitaire et Officier de l'Ordre du Canada, Henry
Kreisel est né à Vienne d'une famille juive en 1922. En 1938, il a
quitté son pays natal pour l'Angleterre et a été interné pendant
dix-huit mois, au Canada, lors de la Seconde Grande Guerre.
Après ses études à l'Université de Toronto, il devint professeur
à l'Université en 1947, et à partir de 1961 jusqu'à 1970, il a dirigé
le département d'anglais. De 1970 à 1975, il a été vice-recteur
(universitaire), et a été nommé professeur hors rang en 1975,
la plus haute distinction scientifique décernée par l'Université
de l'Alberta à un membre de son professorat. Professeur adoré,
il a transmis l'amour de la littérature à plusieurs générations
d'étudiants, et il a été parmi les premiers écrivains modernes
du Canada à aborder l'expérience immigrante. Il est décédé à
Edmonton en 1991. Son œuvre comprend les romans, *The Rich
Man* (1948) et *The Betrayal* (1964), et un recueil de nouvelles
intitulé *The Almost Meeting* (1981). Son journal d'internement,
accompagné d'articles critiques sur ses écrits, paraît dans *Another
Country: Writings by and about Henry Kreisel* (1985).

La générosité de l'enseignement du Professeur Kreisel et
son influence sur la littérature moderne du Canada inspirent
profondément le travail public et scientifique du CLC et son
engagement à l'égard de la diversité et la qualité remarquables
des écrits du Canada. Le Centre adhère à l'importance
qu'accordait de façon inaugurale Henry Kreisel à la connaissance
des littératures de son propre pays. Enfin, le CLC poursuit la

compréhension d'un monde compliqué et difficile qui détermine les littératures canadiennes et qui est bien susceptible de se voir transformé par elles.

DANIEL LAFOREST

Directeur, Centre de littérature canadienne

Edmonton, février 2014

INTRODUCTION

A couple of years ago, in 2011, an extraordinary story unfolded in
Canadian literature as the various prize lists came out: a pair of
relatively unknown writers, Esi Edugyan and Patrick deWitt, were
shortlisted for—everything. All the big Canadian awards: the
Giller Prize, the Governor General's Award, and the Writers Trust.
They both went on to be shortlisted for the Booker Prize—two
Canadians!—and were only knocked out by that über-Englishman,
Julian Barnes.

Esi prevailed in Canada, winning the Giller Prize for *Half-Blood
Blues*, her dazzling reconstruction of jazz musicians riffing in the
shadow of Nazi Germany. The book has continued to rack up
prizes nationally and internationally—it's a long list, so make your-
selves comfortable. *Half-Blood Blues* won the 2011 Scotiabank
Giller Prize, the Ethel Wilson Fiction Prize, and the 2012 Anisfield-
Wolf Book Award, an American prize honouring books which
make important contributions to the understanding of racism.
It was shortlisted for the 2012 Orange Prize for Fiction, now
the Women's Prize, and for the Walter Scott Prize for Historical
Fiction (again, paired with Patrick deWitt).

It has been a great critical success as well, something that
doesn't always follow, making every best book list ever penned,
and most of the bookclub lists tacked up on fridges across the
country. *Half-Blood Blues* has now been published in more than
a dozen countries, and I'm sure there are more to come.

In the middle of all that acclaim and attention and the punishing
tour schedule that prize lists provoke—not unlike Ginger Rogers
doing the same dances as Fred Astaire, only backwards and in
high heels—Esi had a baby.

It's possible that a brand new baby is the best grounding a
writer could ever have. Regardless of the praise heaped upon one

in the outer world, a baby reduces the tinsel to absolute reality: nothing is more vital than getting that baby fed and satisfied— keeping it alive.

Esi sailed through the rapids of that turbulent booktour season with elegance and grace, never seeming fazed or self-satisfied, always gently smiling, always very nicely turned out. Always patient, no matter how inane the interviewer's questions or how long over-time the other panelists read. And the baby flourished. Esi reminded me ruefully that during one of the readings we shared at a writers festival, her daughter cried all through my reading—but I don't remember it that way, and I'm sure nobody in the audience does either. Real life was there along with us, not trumping fiction, but providing living proof of the reason for fiction: the real life that we try to capture.

Although the story of *Half-Blood Blues*'s success has the fragrance of overnight success, in fact Esi Edugyan had been working very hard at fiction for a long time before this book took flight. After studying at Johns Hopkins University and the University of Victoria, she published her first novel, *The Second Life of Samuel Tyne*, about a Ghanaian immigrant who moves to Amber Valley in Alberta to start a new life. The book was published in 2004 in Canada and internationally, and Esi was one of Knopf Canada's New Faces of Fiction.

Then the manuscript of her second novel failed to land a publisher. That's the kind of thing that makes writers think seriously about quitting. But she had a residency to go to at a castle in Stuttgart, Germany, and the remarkable luxury of time to write and think that a residency allows turned into *Half-Blood Blues*.

The novel is set in occupied Paris, where Hiero, a brilliant young musician, is arrested by the Nazis. As well as being guilty of jazz, that degenerate music of blacks and Jews, Hiero is the son of a white German mother and an African soldier, one of the mixed-race Germans who came to be known as "Rhineland bastards," a despised population denied citizenship and persecuted by the Nazis.

The jazz lingo that Esi occupies with such convincing ease gives the book its vivid life and authority, but the language is not just research—it's rooted in the intimate thought pattern of Sid, the narrator. It is his subjective eye and ear, his fear and his passion for music, that pulls us into the world of *Half-Blood Blues*.

I talked to Esi's old friend Jacqueline Baker, the author of the beautiful *Horseman's Graves*, who says that "Esi is one of the kindest, gentlest, most honourable people—and one of the hardest working, most dedicated writers—I've ever known."

Jacquie talked about the difficult times that form a disproportionate part of the writing life. "We'd had some struggles, both of us, trying to get our footing in new projects, and there was a good deal of despair floating around between us. We'd both been working on novels yet to see the light of day...dark, dark times. Then seemingly out of the blue Esi sends me this new manuscript. I opened it and read the opening, which in that version was Sid talking about 'that night' and the Czech and needing to go out for milk...And I was, well, gobsmacked. You know when you read something and you just know, this is it. That voice was gripping. I read the entire manuscript that first day. Even now, I still don't know how she did it, how she got that voice exactly right."

Half-Blood Blues was picked up by Key Porter Books—one step forward—but then publication was delayed when the Key Porter went on permanent hiatus. Two steps back.

Patrick Crean, then at Thomas Allen, was already publishing Esi's husband Steven Price's first novel, *Into That Darkness*, that year. He got the *Half-Blood Blues* manuscript, read it in two sittings, and snatched it up. "It was a slam dunk," he says. "There was the compelling nature of the story—and the editing had already been done. We were a lucky publisher to have this wonderful book land in our lap." As it turned out, they were very lucky.

Esi's Kreisel Lecture explores the concept of home. With the wild success of *Half-Blood Blues*, she has travelled enough in these last few years to have had time to think passionately, in lonely airport lounges and hotel beds, about belonging and home. She's had a lifetime to think about citizenship, and the complicated ways we define where we are from—her parents immigrated to Canada from Ghana, but Esi Edugyan is a Calgary girl, born and raised. She now lives in Victoria, British Columbia, with her husband, the novelist and poet Steven Price, and her lovely young daughter, the seasoned darling of the literary festival circuit.

I invite you to turn the page and travel with her—to enjoy, as the MC says in the clubs, the wonderful jazz stylings of Ms—Esi—Edugyan!

MARINA ENDICOTT
Edmonton, February 2014

Dreaming of Elsewhere

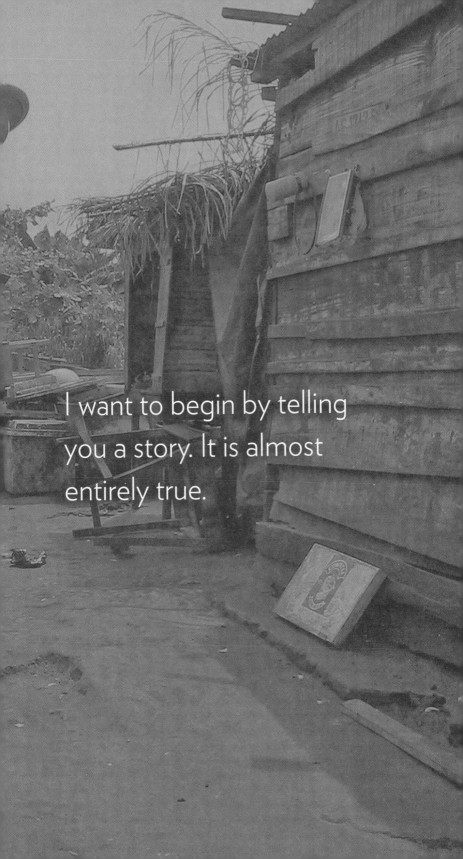

I want to begin by telling you a story. It is almost entirely true.

In 1707, a young boy from the Axim region of what is now Ghana journeyed by caravan to the west coast of Africa, where he was shackled and rowed out to a small trading vessel anchored just outside of the breakers, off the long white beaches there. It must have been his first glimpse of an ocean and a sky vaster and bluer than anything he had known in the riverlands where he had been raised. The boy was taken north to Germany, perhaps as a sold slave, perhaps as a birthday gift for an aristocrat, perhaps as an experiment in education by a preacher in the Dutch West India Company. The reasons are not clear. But once in Germany, he was taken to live at the palace of Duke Anton von Wolfenbuttel, a minor Saxon aristocrat. The boy was christened Anthony Wilhelm Rudolph Amo. We have no idea what name he might have answered to before that moment; but Amo he became, and Amo he is still.

Germany at that time would have meant horses, wheeled carriages, vast public edifices; it would have meant sculpture and churchbells and snow. It would have meant flushed pink faces, elaborate and complicated clothing, pianofortes, face powders. The meat must have been strange, the beer thick and bitter. In the countryside, if the boy were to have stepped from his carriage, the waters would have run very cold, the trees would appear sickly and bared of their leaves. All of this must have struck Amo as terrifying, marvellous, incomprehensible. There is no aloneness quite so stark as genuine unbelonging.

But the duke—something of a maverick, an early enlightenment thinker, and a philanthropist—set out to educate Amo, recognizing the boy's intelligence. Amo proved a quick study. In time he was accepted to the University of Halle, Saxony, writing his dissertation on the rights of Moors in Europe; he would complete his studies at the University of Wittenberg, where his subjects included medicine, physiology, and psychology. By 1727 he had mastered Latin, Dutch, Greek, French, and Hebrew.

Did he belong in the academy? Certainly he did not leave it: he returned to teach at the Universities of Halle, Jana, and

Wittenberg, lecturing in medicine, philosophy, physiology, and the theory of codes. University records of the time remark on his "sheer intelligence, his indefatigability, and dignified comportment, on the scope of his erudition and the brilliance of his lectures." They also remark upon his "outstanding uprightness, his influence on his elders, and his leadership among his peers."[1] By 1733 Amo had secured further degrees, in medicine and science and philosophy; he would in time be invited to act as counsel to the court of Berlin. Surely if belonging could be taught, Amo must have learned it.

In February of 2007 I was in a taxi making my slow way in to Toronto from the airport. The driver was a stout black man heavily bundled in several scarves, wearing gloves with only the fingertips cut out, as one sees drivers do in movies.

We got to talking, and I learned he had been a professor of physics in Accra. He had taught for many years and had published extensively. His classes had been full. He had come here, he said, for the sake of his sons, to offer them a better future.

"Do you miss Ghana?" I asked, thinking of my parents.

"No."

"You don't miss being a professor?"

"Eh, I will not drive a cab forever," he laughed. "I go to night school with my two sons. I have big plans, big plans."

When I think of Amo, I cannot help but think also of this anonymous professor. Three hundred years separate their lives, and so much has changed. And yet the nature of belonging has not. As the daughter of Ghanaian immigrants, raised in a household where Twi, Fante and Asante were as likely to be heard as English or French, my life has been an uneasy one in relation to the ground under my feet. Home, for me, was not a birthright, but an invention.

I would like to talk to you today about the actual and the possible, which is the special territory of fiction. Which is to say, I want to talk about the problem of belonging, of *home*, both as a place and as an idea. It seems to me when we speak of home we are speaking of several things, often at once, muddled together into an uneasy stew. We say *home* and mean origins, we say *home* and mean belonging. These are two different things: where we come from, and where we are.

After the publication of my first novel, *The Second Life of Samuel Tyne*, I was often asked two questions which I found hard to answer: Do I consider my writing to be post-colonial? And: Do I believe we are living in a post-racial age? To both I would shuffle my feet and fumble for an answer. It is awkward for a writer to speak about such things from the inside, as it were. These are not the sorts of concerns one has on one's desk while writing. But if pressed I would say now that I believe the age of post-colonial literature has passed, at least for us. We do not live with an empire exerting its fist over us on a daily basis. Post-colonial narratives were written against, and in the wake of, being silenced. They were an act of self-assertion, a necessary counterweight here in Canada to mainstream stories about a homogenous, particular segment of the population. Post-colonialism encouraged a chorus of voices, where for a long time there had been only one. In other words, it was an explosion of multiplicity. But today, in Canada and Britain and the US, a novel written from a "minority" perspective is hardly controversial. If anything, it has become the new dominant kind of narrative. Publishers seek them out; young writers are encouraged to flaunt their ethnic distinctiveness; reviewers foreground such elements in their reviews. We have entered a different age, a post-post-colonial age. I write with the awareness of those who paved the way, but without the challenge or responsibility of shattering their same barriers. Some doors are still closed to me, certainly; but it is not as it was. It is a different world.

And do I believe that we live in a colour-blind society, a society where race goes unnoticed? I confess I find the notion ridiculous.

We are as we ever were, inclined to quick judgements based on what we see. And all too often what we see are the differences.

Much of the latter part of my twenties was spent seeking out such differences. In the span of five years I lived in or visited Iceland, Scotland, France, Italy, Germany, Holland, Belgium, Hungary, Finland, the US, and Greece. I relished the freedom each trip afforded me, the freedom to be someone other than I was in Canada, leaving myself behind for a month or two at a time. This otherness was rooted, of course, in foreign preconceptions about me, in the ways I was treated and spoken to in each new city. In Paris I became the familiar expat who spoke an inoffensively peculiar French and slunk down from her cheap flat late in the morning for a cup of verveine tea. In Rome I became, through one of those charming misunderstandings, "Assia of Vancouver." In Brussels I was that most annoying of immigrants, who refused to learn *both* of the country's national languages and spoke only a foreigner's French. And in Budapest—a city whose few black people are mostly young men from African countries come to study medicine—I became that most outlandish of strangers, an apparition so dark and odd people in the street sometimes paused to watch me pass.

What was I looking for in those years? Certainly nothing so easy or wrongheaded as a sense of belonging. I still do not know; I suspect it had something to do with finding a perspective on where I had been, rather than on where I was standing. A sort of desire to disorient myself, rather than an attempt to comprehend the world. What I knew was that *I did not know*. Something was unsettled in me.

This unsettling we have come to regard as a peculiarly modern phenomenon. I wonder if this is true. In 1747, when a new hostility towards liberal ideas reared its head in Germany, especially as concerned the rights of Africans in Europe, Amo became the target of a public lampooning at a Halle theatre. The embarrassment appears to have been unusually profound; as a result, Amo abandoned his adopted country and returned to his native Ghana.

It is impossible for us to know how much of this was a leavetaking for Amo, and how much a return. He had lived for nearly half a century in a world of scientific discovery, of stratified social hierarchies, of multilingual histories and weather and plants and foodstuffs entirely foreign to the land of his birth. I wonder if he appeared a lonely man, in his late age, saddened by his exile, or a man joyful and relieved of a heavy burden. What is known is that he was received as something of an oracle by his villagers upon his return. And he did move back in to live with his father and grown sister—strangers both, one imagines—for in 1753 the Dutch took him from his home for a second time, and transferred him east to Fort San Sebastian. This was no doubt done to contain the circulation of his dangerous ideas—his criticisms of slavery, his endorsements of formal education, his condemnation of superstition. At San Sebastian he lived out his last days in solitude and silence.

I do not wish to suggest Amo's fate was to be the pawn of colonial forces, though there is truth in this, certainly. My interest is in what sort of complex feelings he must have had towards the several places he had lived. In other words, my interest is in the fiction of his life, the man he was on the inside, those elements of what we are that are lost to history and recoverable only through storytelling, until the man and the character both live only in narrative itself. This is another kind of uprootedness, one in which we, as storytelling animals, are all complicit. The Amo that I recall here, just like the anonymous taxi driver in Toronto, is a fiction. The few facts that we have are not sufficient to bring us truly closer to a life so unlike our own.

The African-American writer James Baldwin wrestled with this very problem of *unalikeness* his entire life. He left New York for Paris in the spring of 1948 and lived the rest of his life in Europe. He did not set out to *arrive* in one particular place, but rather to *leave* another; belonging was a thing he would not ever know. The Swiss, he wrote,

> move with an authority which I shall never have; and they regard me, quite rightly, not only as a stranger in their village but as a suspect latecomer, bearing no credentials, to everything they have—however unconsciously—inherited. For this village, even were it incomparably more remote and incredibly more primitive, is the West, the West onto which I have been so strangely grafted. These people cannot be, from the point of view of power, strangers anywhere in the world; they have made the modern world, in effect, even if they do not know it. The most illiterate among them is related, in a way that I am not, to Dante, Shakespeare, Michelangelo, Aeschylus, Da Vinci, Rembrandt, and Racine; the cathedral at Chartres says something to them which it cannot say to me, as indeed would New York's Empire State Building should anyone here ever see it. Out of their hymns and dances come Beethoven and Bach. Go back a few centuries and they are in their full glory—but I am in Africa, watching the conquerors arrive.[2]

It amazes me to think this could be Amo speaking, in a soft voice, from out of his own era. This could be that taxi driver I'd met in Toronto. This could have been me.

Home is the first exile. To belong in one place is to not belong in another. And for those of us uneasy in our own skins, for those of us who have arrived in a new place, whether during our own lifetimes or by virtue of being the first of a generation born into a new land, a new language, a new identity, it is difficult to ignore the creeping suspicion that we are not wholly *here*, that some part of us is not still *over there*—wherever that "there" might be. Travelling in Europe in my twenties, during my graduate work in Baltimore, throughout my childhood in Calgary, I would often be asked where I'd come from.

"Canada," I would reply, and then brace for the inevitable next question.

"Yes—but where are you from *really?*"

This brings me to the kind of belonging with which I have been most concerned recently, that of citizenship.

The *Oxford English Dictionary* defines a citizen as, "an inhabitant, possessing civic rights and privileges." That this is not always true should come as no surprise. Citizenship is, in the end, an expression of power. Our First Nations communities have felt this assertion directly, as have our separatists in Québec. Conflicts, one would suppose, are inevitable. But among the many modern examples of nations in conflict with their own citizens, I suspect the abrupt rise and fall of Nazi Germany is most instructive. There are many others, of course: Cambodia, China, the USSR, the United States, to name just a few. Yet Nazi Germany casts a peculiar spell over us, even eight decades later. Historians continue to debate how such a movement came to be embraced. The most reductive simply shrugging, as if to point to humanity's rather ugly inclination towards aggression, tribalism, or exclusion as some kind of answer. I'm not convinced that this is adequate. And all the while the Third Reich continues to fascinate us with the mysterious ferocity of its evil.

I have been struggling with this for several years. What, I have wondered, was a German citizen in 1932? And what was a German citizen in 1933? The human beings were the same. And yet the citizens were already startlingly, if secretively, different. Germany did not eradicate its own citizens. That would have been appalling. Instead they denied them. Then they eradicated them. My second novel, *Half-Blood Blues*, explores the fate of one such citizen, Hieronymous Falk, a black German jazz trumpeter, at his peak during the rise of the Third Reich, and my interest in Falk grew quite naturally out of my own life. As James Baldwin once wrote, rather bleakly, "People are trapped in history, and history is trapped in them."

But more about that shortly.

In 2006, I had already been living in Stuttgart for several months before I came across a reference to the "Rhineland Bastards." These were the children of white German mothers and black French colonial soldiers, born during and after France's occupation of the Rhineland in the years immediately following the First World War. Some of the German populace saw the use of black soldiers as a deliberate insult, an attempt to taint the bloodline. The children must have felt that sting. The book I had been reading was interested in the aftermath of that first war, not in the fates of the Rhineland Bastards. A short while later, as I was on the bus returning home, a black woman struggled to get onto the bus with her several shopping bags. The driver—with the aggression so many bus drivers in that city seemed to possess—at once began furiously berating her. She glanced up at him, and said four sharp words back. The bus driver immediately lowered his voice, and replied to her in a respectful tone. I do not know what she said; I do not know what he felt. But she paid her fare, the doors slid shut, and he waited until she had sat down before pulling from the curb. I was watching this black woman who spoke such elegant German, and all at once I wondered what had happened to those children from the Rhineland as they grew up.

The fate of black Germans under the Third Reich is a topic of which very little has been written. This is due to several reasons. Firstly, there were not many of them, relatively speaking. Secondly, their fate has been obscured by several of the more overwhelming tragedies of that era. Thirdly, so much legislative confusion abounded as to what was to be done with black citizens, that their treatment often seems puzzling or contradictory to us in hindsight.

For instance, the children of African diplomats who had come to Germany during its colonial period were mostly left alone; it seems German authorities wanted to maintain a good reputation on that continent in order to win back their lost colonies. Some Afro-Germans who could not find work would be reduced to poverty, while only a few kilometres away other Afro-Germans would continue to run successful shops, or work as well-paid master craftsmen. Several Africans continued to teach at schools, long after Jewish employees had been fired. Throughout the Reich, citizens of mixed heritage were forcefully sterilized, but otherwise permitted to go free. In a few isolated cases, to my astonishment, I learned black children had even been accepted into the Hitler Youth.

One such child who survived the war, and who was later interviewed on this subject by the historian Tina Campt, was the man known as "Peter K." He was sterilized around the time he turned 15; for him it proved a revelation to the reality of Nazism. Being a member of the Hitler Youth, whatever other comforts it might have provided, had until that moment had material benefits even for an Afro-German. As he admitted, "I was an apprentice with the railroad. Without being in the Hitler Youth, I wouldn't have been allowed to do that." This was not the only benefit. Only those in the Hitler Youth were allowed to graduate to secondary school; and failure to join served as an invitation to harrassment and physical assault. Wearing the uniform of the Hitler Youth was, in Peter K's experience, a new kind of skin, neither black nor white: simply German.

In *Half-Blood Blues*, Heironymous Falk feels a similar pressure, a similar desire to be absorbed into the larger German idea of itself. How can one feel oneself to be German, or even Canadian, for that matter, if one is denied public enfranchisement? The physical differences between the characters in my novel gradually began, for me, to become entangled with their sense of identity, as their freedoms were curtailed or widened accordingly. Sid Griffiths, a light-skinned African-American, can walk freely through the streets of Berlin without dread; Chip Jones, his darker-skinned friend from Baltimore, cannot. Paul, the band's pianist, is an Aryan in everything but blood: blonde, blue-eyed, and Jewish. Hieronymous, as a black German, is declared a "stateless" person and denied citizenship in his own country. No man among them is allowed to be his authentic self. It was Hieronymous, most interestingly to me, who surprised me with the passion of his patriotism. He feels a deep-seated sense of Germanness, an intensity that perplexes the other characters. In Hamburg he tells Sid:

> My daddy...he a chief in Douala. Here he just a savage in civilized clothes. But hell, Sid...I ain't never heard him say a damn word against Germany. Not once. Herodotus tell this story bout King Darius of Persia. The king called the Greeks to him and asked, How much scratch I got to pay you to eat the bodies of you fathers when they die? Greeks told him ain't no sum on earth get them do that. Then Darius called some Indians to him, jacks who eat their fathers, and asked them in front of the Greeks, How much scratch I got to pay you to burn the bodies of you fathers when they die? Indians said no way in hell they burn their fathers. See, a jack always reckon his own customs is the best in the world. Ain't no way you change his mind. But my daddy, he wasn't like that. He come to Germany, that be it. He make hisself into a German.[3]

I do not know if it is possible to "make" oneself into anything. There are so many elements of which we have so little control and which affect and alter our place in this life. But the lack of cohesion in Nazi Germany's policies reflected a fracture buried but still present, even at its outset, a tearing of itself at its very centre. What does it mean to belong? If the Third Reich speaks to this problem at all, it must be to warn against a simple "us" vs.

"them" manner of thinking. If differences were going to be what determined us, that is, where one of us ended and another began, then what of the power of alikeness: what purpose might *it* serve?

During that year in Stuttgart several coincidences came together—it does not matter what they were—and I found myself suddenly astonished, realizing I must take yet another trip, this time to Ghana, to the home of my parents, to meet my dying grandmother in her hometown of Kumasi.

I had never set foot in Africa in my life. Ghana had never been my true inheritance; after all, I had not grown up speaking Twi, Fante or Asante, though my parents had spoken all among themselves and their friends; and I had never met any of my forty-three aunts and uncles, let alone the hundreds of cousins. Nevertheless I knew this trip would be, in some ways, a kind of return.

That Lufthansa flight would prove unlike any other I had taken. In the crowd of mostly black passengers, I felt weirdly diminished, as if some of my edges had blurred, fallen away. Everyone seemed to make themselves pleasantly at home at 34,000 feet—we might have been gathered in someone's living room, or a local marketplace. Strangers laughed and teased each other in the aisles; when the snacks were distributed, loud arguments erupted over who should get the pretzel mix, who the oatmeal cookies. More than one passenger tried to barter down the price on the duty-free goods. A woman to my left cried out, "Eh, give me two for one!" During a stopover in Lagos, as the plane taxied in slow rotations on the dark tarmac, the man sitting next to me sucked his teeth. "Are we going to *drive* the rest of the way or what?"

Though I did not realize it, I was in Ghana already.

In the customs lineup in Accra, I understood I'd forgotten to bring the address of the person with whom I would be staying. Because I had convinced my sister and brother to join me in

Ghana, and their flights had brought them in some days before, I knew they would be waiting outside to pick me up. The young customs agent merely shook her head. "Well, go out there and get the address from them," she said.

"What, just go on through?"

"Yes. I will keep your passport."

"Should I leave my luggage?"

"No. Take it through with you."

I paused. Then slowly, watching her face, I began to make my way through the gates, waiting for her to call me back. But she'd already moved on to the next person in line. I rushed through the terminal, and made my way outside, thinking, *I could just leave, I could just disappear.*

Later, in the taxi with my brother and sister, I had my first real glimpse of the country my parents had left. The air burned with car exhaust; a wall of heat, heavy with chemicals, seemed to press in from all sides, even inside the taxi. We passed people hawking toilet paper and shrink-wrapped apples in the middle of the highway, cars swerving around them. Women strolled roadside, carrying huge carafes on their heads. Cars sped up and stopped abruptly, signalling left not to tell you they were turning, but to warn you it was unsafe to pass. Closer to town, we began to read out the storefronts: To Be A Man Is Not Easy Haircut. Fred's Tact Shop. God Is Great Fast Food. No Bad Deed Goes Unpunished Vulcanizing Service. A lorry sped by, a cardboard sign on its back christening it The Glorry. Suddenly, the driver wrenched to the right, stopping along the shoulder. Stepping from his rig, he lowered to his knees, pressing his forehead into the dust. It was the hour of prayer, and nothing, least of all this irritating afternoon traffic, would stop him from observing it.

Above all of it, like a clean sheet of salt, stretched a painful bright white sky.

Our host in Accra, Kojo, was a man of some dubious relation to our mother. He might have been a cousin; he might have been a childhood friend; he might have been simply a fellow villager. Ties of friendship are common enough among Ghanaians, and in many cases just as important as blood. Kojo was a stout, round-headed soul with ears that bent away from his head like two fins. He greeted us at the door with grandiose gestures and a rush of laughter. "So you're here!" he cried, laughing and laughing. "And for so long a visit! So long! Did you say you are leaving, what, the twenty-fourth?"

Kojo lived in company housing on the outskirts of the city. He was also, he explained as soon as we sat down, building a house in the country. "It has twelve rooms and indoor toilets, many, many toilets," he said, looking modestly away. "It is not finished yet."

Whether blood or not, I could see my own features in his. I sensed my brother and sister doing it too, searching for resemblances. Kojo was short, stocky, with a spare face whose Asiatic eyes fixed you very sharply. It felt perplexing, almost stupefying, to find the echo of our own selves in a complete stranger, as if some part of us had been waiting for us to arrive all these years.

Despite our protests, Kojo insisted he drive us north to Kumasi to meet our grandmother. "We shall all go," he said, pursing his lips. "You will enjoy it. I have BMW."

That night my sister and I lay in the darkened guest room, whispering about our grandmother, about Kojo, about the drive to Kumasi. My sister mentioned how surprised she was by Kojo's status consciousness. "All that stuff about being top management and maybe building a second house." She found it sad and embarrassing. We slept.

Three hours later I woke in alarm. The darkness was muggy, smelling of soil. Someone beside me gasped. It was my sister. Of course. Of course. We were in Ghana.

This happened nearly every night of that trip: one of us would lurch awake, startling the other from sleep. For the first few nights in Accra a mean-spirited rooster outside of our window would begin to crow at 2 A.M., punctually, in the darkness. Much later, in Kumasi, a muezzin's call to prayer would startle us, his ghostly voice drifting over the streets.

When we lit out for Kumasi, Kojo insisted my brother sit beside him in the front. As he merged onto the highway, Kojo turned the volume up on his favourite gospel cassette, then almost immediately began yelling over the music.

"So when do you three move back?" he shouted.

I glanced at my sister, as if seeking a tactful response.

The gospel music crooned. *Are you free from the curses of your ancestors?*

Kojo leaned towards my brother in the passenger seat. "You will return to be chief of your father's village," he hollered. My father is descended from a line of minor chiefs in Gomua-Kumasi down south; my brother could return to claim that inheritance.

My brother said nothing.

Are you free from the curses of your past?

Kojo sucked his teeth, his voice growing peevish. "You could have it so, so easy if you would come here." He shook his head steadily. "You would not have to lift a finger, man. They would carry you everywhere on their shoulders. You could have every woman you want." He began to speak of our parents' departure from this country as though it were an aberration. "You could have it all back," he yelled. "Everything."

Are you free from the curses of your ancestors?

"What's this music?" I said.

"McAbraham," said Kojo, as though everyone should know this.

Are you free from the curses of your past?

"What other tapes do you have?"

Kojo jabbed at the eject button with a thick thumb, the music stopping hard. He did not put in another cassette. We had just passed a gaudily dressed woman walking along the shoulder of the road and Kojo barked out a scornful laugh. "These Nigerians," he said. "Such a dirty way of dressing."

My sister grimaced. "How could you even tell she was Nigerian? We didn't see her for two seconds."

"Who but a Nigerian would dress like that?"

And on Kojo went, cheerful in his bigotry. If not the Nigerians, then "the damned French," by whom he meant not the French from France, but Africans from the old French colonies. He railed against university students who left their country and never came back, abandoning their countrymen rather than sharing their learning; he screamed about the children of such traitors who dared to return "like tourists" before leaving again; and finally he dressed down people who insisted on being driven all around the country "like no one else has anything better to do."

"They deserve to be bankrupted," he finished, his voice falling. "They deserve it."

"Bankrupted?" I said. "What do you mean?"

But he did not answer.

A few minutes later, when my sister needed to use the restroom, we stopped at a roadside restaurant. She returned to the car complaining of the hygiene.

Twisting his mouth, Kojo started the car. "Eh, you kids," he spat. "You are home now. If you are going to be living here, you have got to learn how it is done here."

Home. Kojo's was an easy assumption, though it perplexed me at the time. It had to do with a kind of tribal inclusion, a bond of blood and history which did not require mutual consent. It was enough for my relatives—distant strangers, all—to regard me and my siblings as a part of their world. It mattered not at all that we resisted such inclusion, that we turned from their world which felt to us so alien. I realize now that our sudden waking each night had nothing to do with an aggressive rooster, or a muezzin's call to prayer. We were simply, profoundly, not at our ease. We did not belong.

Not-belonging is so often rooted in difference that we forget, sometimes, that it can be rooted in similarities as well. I remember being in a large plaza of shops in Accra before our journey north to Kumasi. In the dusty, unpaved lot I saw, against the far stalls, two tall pale figures. They were blonde. Sewn into their backpacks were two tiny red maple leaves.

"Look," I said to my brother, and pointed.

After just three days in Ghana, a glimpse of white skin—so much a part of my home landscape, a part of what I had always known in the world I came out of—could startle me. I had recently read a biography of the nineteenth-century Welsh explorer Henry Morton Stanley, and I was reminded of a passage Stanley had written about seeing two white men at the Portuguese trading post of Boma after spending months in the African interior:

> *The pale colour, after so long gazing on rich black and richer bronze, had something of an unaccountable ghastliness. I could not divest myself of the feeling that they must be sick...Yet there was something very self-possessed about the carriage of these whites...the calm blue-grey eyes rather awed me, and the immaculate purity of their clothes dazzled me.*[4]

Hieronymous, too, would have lived in that shadowy space between belonging and not-belonging. As one of a growing group of exiles and "stateless" persons, he would have had little in common with his fellows beyond a shared "broken citizenship"— by which I mean a severing of genuine belonging. At festivals and readings I am sometimes asked how I came to inhabit a character so seemingly removed from myself. Perhaps it should not seem so strange to us. But I myself was surprised to realize, late in the writing of *Half-Blood Blues*, that I was drawing on that journey to Ghana taken in my twenty-ninth year. Though the circumstances could not have been more different, I too had felt that dizzying feeling of not-belonging in a place where everything is at once both strange and familiar.

I, who had lived so much of my life looking elsewhere, was slowly coming to acknowledge that not-belonging, also, can be a kind of belonging. There are all sorts of nations on this earth. It is a lonelier citizenship, perhaps, but a vast one.

3

When *Half-Blood Blues* was published in the fall of 2011, one of the criticisms levelled against it in the Canadian press was the wearying complaint that, once again, a Canadian novelist had set her story in the past, and abroad—

as if by doing so I had refused to engage with what it means to be a contemporary Canadian. I confess I found the complaint puzzling.

The assumption that I should, as a citizen of a given nation, tell certain stories instead of others, is a dubious one at best. For who is to say which stories will matter to us? Who is to say what a Canadian story looks like, where it should be set, who should be telling it? What language should it be told in? Indeed, what is a Canadian at all, what does one of this peculiar breed look like, how can we be certain that what we have before us is indeed a Canadian? Check its passport?

I said little about this at the time, but let me speak to it now. The stories we tell, in our own voices, are Canadian by virtue of, well, us. The concerns we have, whatever they are, however removed they may be, are Canadian by the same right. Nationhood, as we think of it today, is an idea not much more than 200 years old; already in our ever-shrinking world it feels

somewhat musty and faded at the seams, confused by matters of
identity, race, geography, language. And how does belonging fit
into this? Is it simply a matter of citizenship? Is it even up to us?

The first person of African descent to set foot on Canadian
soil, or the soil we would one day call Canadian, arrived in 1603
with Champlain. He was a freeman named Mathieu da Costa.
"Freeman" was an important designation; any black person not
legally "freed" was by default a slave. A translator, da Costa spoke
Dutch, English, French, Portuguese, and Basque, which was
the dialect used by many First Nations peoples in their trading
encounters with Europeans. The first person of African descent
to live in Canada was an anonymous man who died of scurvy
in Port-Royal during the winter of 1606–1607. But the first we
know by name was a slave from Madagascar, Olivier le Jeune,
who lived in Québec and belonged to Guillaume Couillard.
Slavery was not legalized in New France until 1709, but this means
nothing; le Jeune may or may not have died a free man. What is

known is that he was chained up for twenty-four hours in 1638 for slandering a man; he signed his confession with an X. He was dead by the age of thirty. The first black Canadian? In 1867 there were some 40,000 blacks in Canada. They were Confederated, just like the land was, though they too had no vote in the outcome. My own bloodline arrived in Edmonton shortly after the Confederation centennial celebrations.

One of the reasons I wanted to talk about the idea of home was to explore some of my own uneasy, troubled thoughts on the topic. What does it mean to walk down the vast, wintery streets of Toronto and know that no part of you had a hand in what looms there? I stand before the museums and public statues of Ottawa knowing that no one in my family is represented in such edifices. The wars they fought were elsewhere. The causes they believed in are utterly alien. The laws I obey, the borders of the country I occupy, all were determined by others, by people who were here before I or any of my bloodline had arrived. And that is the crux of it. The roots do not go deep; the past is not one's own. Having been born here, I feel as much a Canadian as anyone. I believe we live only this one life, and are here only a brief time, and that we can claim no credit for what was built before us. But when I look to my parents, their lives straddled two worlds. And the break there is still fresh.

How amazing it was to see my grandmother's village. We climbed from Kojo's BMW on the outskirts and walked through the dusty heat. Men, women, children all poured out of their houses to follow us in a growing procession to the courtyard. Then, at last, our grandmother was carried out to us. A very small, frail woman, toothless, sightless, dressed all in white. It was like seeing a ghost. We were invited to crowd in around her, and she sang to us our names and her childhood songs and we called out to her,

"Nana!" between her chants. It was said she was 102 years old, though no one could be certain, and her jokes and gentle chiding seemed very clear and sharp. Finally she began to sing to us with great seriousness. A man from the village explained her songs to us: that she missed us; that she didn't want us to marry Canadians, but Ghanaians; that she needed more eye medication. She ended with a lengthy prayer for us. And the village stood around us, listening and watching with strangely hopeful eyes, as if wanting to be recognized, singled-out, *noticed*. Everyone wanted their picture taken. Two of the older children sidled up shyly, and when we turned to play with them, other mothers shoved *their* children into our midst, that we might play with them too. I wondered if this would be a story they grew up hearing. Someone slashed the tops off coconuts so we could drink the milk. There was laughter and more singing. Looking at my sister, I could see from the gleam in her face, the utter wonderment and joy, that she was thinking, *I'm home now, I'm home*.

Just then one of the smiling women leaned over to me and yelled, through her beautiful white teeth, "Eh, Obruni, why don't you come home?" and she held me in her strong arms. I could smell the flour in her soft, warm skin. *Come* home, she'd said. Not *go* home.

It wasn't until later that I learned obruni meant White Person.

All our stories are about home. It is our beginning and our ending. And because stories are life, and our lives are not only what we have done and will do, but also what we might have done, the idea of "home" includes, as it must, both departures and arrivals. Every farewell carries the promise of a return. And since I am a novelist, and a firm believer in the power of stories to affect and alter the realities of our world, I believe stories set abroad and stories set in one's own home serve much the same purpose: to explore what it means to be alive in the present moment, that is, in the current.

I do not think home is a place, only. Nor do I think belonging is the most important of our possibilities, long for it though we might. I believe home is a *way* of thinking, an *idea* of belonging, which matters more to us than the thing itself. Where we are, who we are, who we are with: these are so intertwined as to be inseparable. What we owe to ourselves we owe to others.

We have always dreamed of elsewheres. It is our privilege as creatures of language who exist within a narrative space, that is, who are trapped inside time. And it is our responsibility, as well. We owe it to each other to struggle to see past those differences which separate us. "Where are you from, *really*?" Here. If every act of empathy is a leaving of the self, then such journeys are more necessary than ever in this world. Dreaming of elsewheres is one of the ways we struggle with the challenge of what it means to be *here*—by which I mean at home, in ourselves.

We leave in order to come back, changed. Made new.

NOTES

1. Robert L. Arrington, ed., *A Companion to Philosophers* (London: Blackwell, 2001), 3.

2. James Baldwin, "Stranger in the Village," in *Collected Essays* (Library of America: New York, 1998), 121.

3. Esi Edugyan, *Half-Blood Blues: A Novel* (Toronto: Thomas Allen, 2011), 153.

4. Qtd in Tim Jeal, *Stanley: The Impossible Life of Africa's Greatest Explorer* (New Haven: Yale University Press, 2007), 213.

BIBLIOGRAPHY

Arrington, Robert L., ed. *A Companion to Philosophers*. London: Blackwell, 2001.

Baldwin, James. *Collected Essays*. Library of America: New York, 1998.

Edugyan, Esi. *Half-Blood Blues: A Novel*. Toronto: Thomas Allen, 2011.

Jeal, Tim. *Stanley: The Impossible Life of Africa's Greatest Explorer*. New Haven: Yale University Press, 2007.

Lusane, Clarence. *Hitler's Black Victims: The Historical Experiences of Afro-Germans, European Blacks, Africans, and African Americans in the Nazi Era*. London: Routledge, 2003.

HENRY KRIESEL LECTURE SERIES

FROM MUSHKEGOWUK TO NEW ORLEANS
A Mixed Blood Highway
Joseph Boyden
ISBN 978-1-897126-29-5

THE OLD LOST LAND OF NEWFOUNDLAND
Family, Memory, Fiction, and Myth
Wayne Johnston
ISBN 978-1-897126-35-6

UN ART DE VIVRE PAR TEMPS DE CATASTROPHE
Dany Laferrière
ISBN 978-0-88864-553-1

THE SASQUATCH AT HOME
Traditional Protocols & Modern Storytelling
Eden Robinson
ISBN 978-0-88864-559-3

IMAGINING ANCIENT WOMEN
Annabel Lyon
ISBN 978-0-88864-629-3

DEAR SIR, I INTEND TO BURN YOUR BOOK
An Anatomy of a Book Burning
Lawrence Hill
ISBN 978-0-88864-679-8.

DREAMING OF ELSEWHERE
Observations on Home
Esi Edugyan
ISBN 978-0-88864-821-1

UNDERSTANDING EACH OTHER
The Essential Importance of Multilingualism
through the Prism of Cree, French, and English
Tomson Highway
coming 2015